TinkerActive

WORKBOOKS

1ST GRADE · SCIENCE · AGES 6–7

by Megan Hewes Butler

illustrated by Lauren Pettapiece and Les McClaine

educational consulting by Amanda Raupe

Odd Dot · New York

Earth

Earth is the planet we live on. It is made of rock and surrounded by air. There is land and water. Color the land green. Color the water blue.

land

water

water

Water collects in oceans, lakes, rivers, and even waterfalls! What bodies of water do you see near your home or neighborhood?

_____

_____

_____

_____

Earth's surface has the air, water, and dirt that plants, animals, and people need to live. Circle the living things. Then draw yourself on Earth's surface.

Look around your home. What living things do you see?

_____

_____

_____

_____

Read the text aloud. Then circle the correct label for each picture.

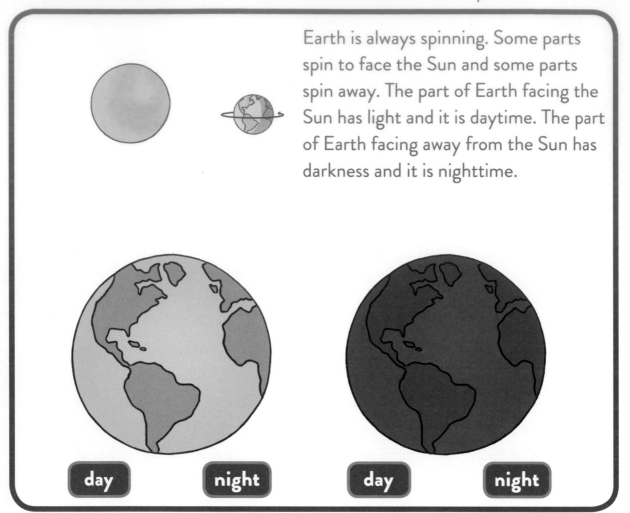

Earth is always spinning. Some parts spin to face the Sun and some parts spin away. The part of Earth facing the Sun has light and it is daytime. The part of Earth facing away from the Sun has darkness and it is nighttime.

day   night   day   night

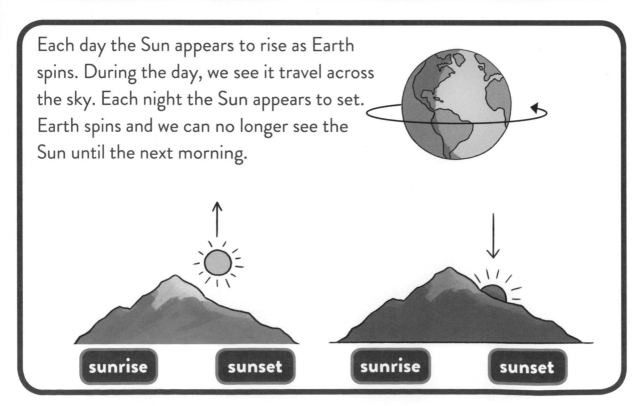

Each day the Sun appears to rise as Earth spins. During the day, we see it travel across the sky. Each night the Sun appears to set. Earth spins and we can no longer see the Sun until the next morning.

sunrise   sunset   sunrise   sunset

Draw lines to connect each activity to the time of day it usually occurs.

day

night

Earth travels around the Sun once per year. The path it moves on is called its orbit. The way the Sun's rays hit Earth as it orbits gives us seasons.

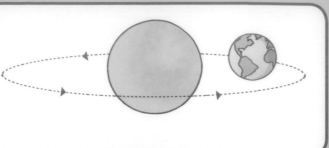

Direct, strong rays cause hotter temperatures in the summer, when days are longer.

Less direct, weaker rays cause colder temperatures in the winter, when days are shorter.

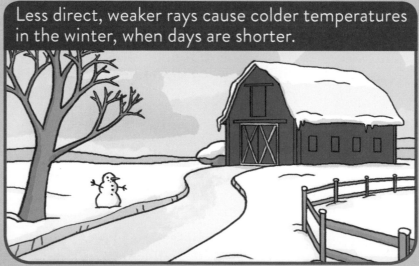

Different locations on Earth have their seasons at different times based on the tilt of Earth toward or away from the Sun. Seasons repeat at the same times every year. It takes 365 days for Earth to orbit the Sun one time.

Circle the correct words in each sentence.

In the summer, the days are **long** / **short**.
In the winter, the days are **long** / **short**.
The seasons happen at **the same time** / **different times** every year.

Every year, the seasons repeat: summer, fall, winter, and spring.

Look out your window. What season is it now? Write about or draw how you know what season it is.

How do you dress for this season? Draw the clothes you wear.

What season is coming next where you live?

_____

LET'S START!

GATHER THESE TOOLS AND MATERIALS.

5 or more rocks

4–6 leaves

4–6 sticks

Trowel

Paper plate

4–6 toothpicks

Shoebox

LET'S TINKER!

There are many patterns on Earth, like day and night, sunrise and sunset, and the seasons.

Create patterns with your materials. Which materials can you repeat? Can you make short patterns? Can you make long patterns?

LET'S MAKE: SUNDIAL!

Earth is always spinning, so the Sun's rays hit it differently throughout the day. **Make** a sundial, which is a simple device for telling time by watching shadows move as Earth spins!

1. On a sunny day, **dig** a small hole in the dirt and **place** one end of a stick in the ground, pointing straight up.

2. **Use** one of your objects, like a rock, to mark where the stick's shadow is on the ground.

3. **Predict** where you think the shadow will be in 10 minutes, 1 hour, much later in the day, and tomorrow morning. **Use** other objects to mark where you think the shadow will move to.

4. **Check** your sundial at different points in the day. Were your predictions correct? Did you observe any patterns? Where did the shadow move to?

LET'S ENGINEER!

Frank's class is getting an insect as a new pet! But it's a surprise— no one knows exactly what kind of insect it will be.

How can Frank provide his new pet with everything it needs to survive when he doesn't know what kind it is?

Set up a habitat with things an insect would need to survive. Use your shoebox as a home. Which materials can be used to make a shelter? Can any of your materials work as food? Where can you put the water?

Look for other materials around your home that can help.

PROJECT 1: DONE!
Get your sticker!

Solar System

Earth is a planet in our solar system. Our solar system is made up of the Sun, eight planets and their moons, and other, smaller objects like asteroids, meteoroids, and comets.

Sun

Circle Earth. How do you know it's Earth?

_____

Using the stickers on page 129, show the Moon orbiting Earth. Draw arrows to show how Earth is spinning.

What is at the center of our solar system? _____. Put the correct sticker from page 129 on it.

asteroid

planets

Draw an X on the largest object in our solar system.

comet

Earth is the only planet with one moon. Jupiter and Saturn each have over fifty moons!

Earth is one of the eight planets that orbit our Sun. Each of these planets is unique. Here are the planets in order from closest to the Sun to farthest from the Sun.

Mercury—the closest planet to the Sun. Mercury is also the smallest planet in our solar system.

Venus—the brightest planet in the sky. Venus's thick clouds reflect lots of light. You can sometimes see Venus from Earth during the day!

Earth—the only planet known to have life on it: plants, animals, and people. We live on Earth!

Mars—a rusty red planet. Iron on Mars's surface rusts, giving the planet its color.

Jupiter—the largest planet in our solar system. Jupiter is over 300 times larger than Earth!

Saturn—the planet with the most rings. Saturn has seven ring groups, each of which is made up of thousands of smaller rings. You can even see them from Earth!

Uranus—the planet tipped over on its side. Uranus spins in such a way that its north and south poles face the Sun as it orbits.

Neptune—the farthest planet from the Sun. It was also the last one to be discovered. It takes 165 Earth years for Neptune to orbit the Sun.

Write the name of each planet in our solar system. Then say the names aloud, from the planet closest to the Sun to the planet farthest from the Sun.

On Earth, we have earthquakes.
But on Mars, there are marsquakes!

Draw a line to match each object to the correct definition.

The **Sun** is the biggest object in our solar system. It is a star—a hot ball of burning gas.

A **planet** is an object in space that moves around a star. Saturn is a planet that orbits the Sun.

A **comet** is a frozen object made of ice and dust that orbits the Sun. It can have a tail.

A **moon** is an object in space that orbits a planet.

An **asteroid** is a jagged object made mostly of rock and metal that orbits the Sun.

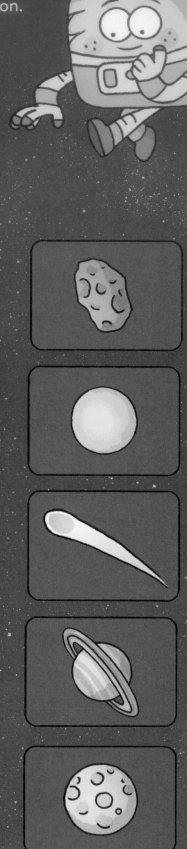

A scientist who studies space is called an astronomer. A telescope is one of the tools an astronomer uses to see objects that are far away in space.

Write about and draw what you'd like to see using a telescope. You can also use stickers from page 129.

LET'S START!

Paper plate

4–6 rocks

4–6 cotton balls

4–6 buttons

Crayons

4–6 rubber bands

Tape or glue

4–6 coins

Construction paper

LET'S TINKER!

Our solar system is filled with objects that are on the move. Comets and asteroids are flying through space. All the planets, including Earth, are spinning as they orbit the Sun.

Spin your materials. Can any of them spin around or fly? What happens if they run into one another?

LET'S MAKE: YOUR OWN PLANET!

Use the materials to make your own made-up planet.

1. Pick a round object, like a paper plate, as the base for your planet.

2. Color your planet with crayons.

3. Give your planet rings or craters. **Name** your planet!

LET'S ENGINEER!

Brian is studying the solar system and wants to remember the order of the eight planets. He knows that Mercury comes first, but what comes next?

How can Brian remember all the planets in order?

Make a model of the eight planets in order. **Design** a way to remember their names. Which planets are small and which are large? Can you add the Sun to your model?

PROJECT 2: DONE!
Get your sticker!

Sun, Moon & Stars

There is only one star in our solar system—the Sun. It is a ball of burning gases that provides the light and heat we need to survive on Earth. Even though it is far away, the Sun is so bright that we cannot look directly at it. Its rays are so powerful that we have to protect our skin so it doesn't burn.

Circle the things you use to protect yourself from the Sun's rays.

The Sun is always shining, but we cannot always see it because Earth spins. When the part of Earth that we are on is facing the Sun, it is day. When the part of Earth that we are on rotates away from the Sun, it is night.

Color the side of Earth reached by the Sun's rays yellow. Color the side of Earth that no light is reaching black.

Read the poem aloud.

Phases of the Moon

Some planets have many moons
and some have none.
On Earth we are lucky—
we have one!

Our moon circles Earth
on a month-long path.
We call this an orbit—
now comes the math.

The Sun shines upon the Moon
and lights up different places.
Each new look has a name—
we call them the Moon's phases!

A full moon shows its whole face.
A new moon hides its light.
A half-moon is half-shadowed,
while the other half is bright.

The Moon is waxing when it's growing
and waning when it's not.
It's crescent when there's less than half
and gibbous when there's a lot.

The phase of the Moon is always changing,
and now that you know the reasons,
you can watch and track the patterns,
even through the seasons!

Color the phases of the Moon that we see from Earth. Use yellow to color the parts of the Moon lit up by the Sun. Use black to color the parts of the Moon we cannot see.

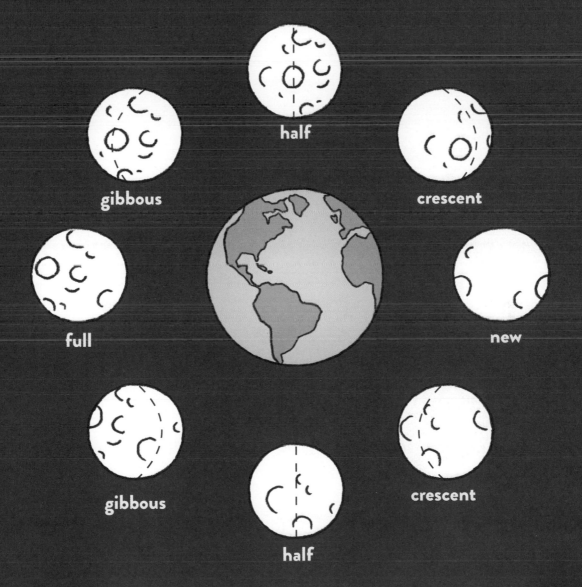

half

gibbous

crescent

full

new

gibbous

crescent

half

Look out your window at night. Can you see the Moon? Which phase is it in?

_____

Stars are balls of burning gases. Groups of stars in a pattern can form a constellation. Connect the dots to form constellations.

Draw what you see outside your window at night. Can you find a constellation? If so, draw it. If not, draw your own pattern of stars.

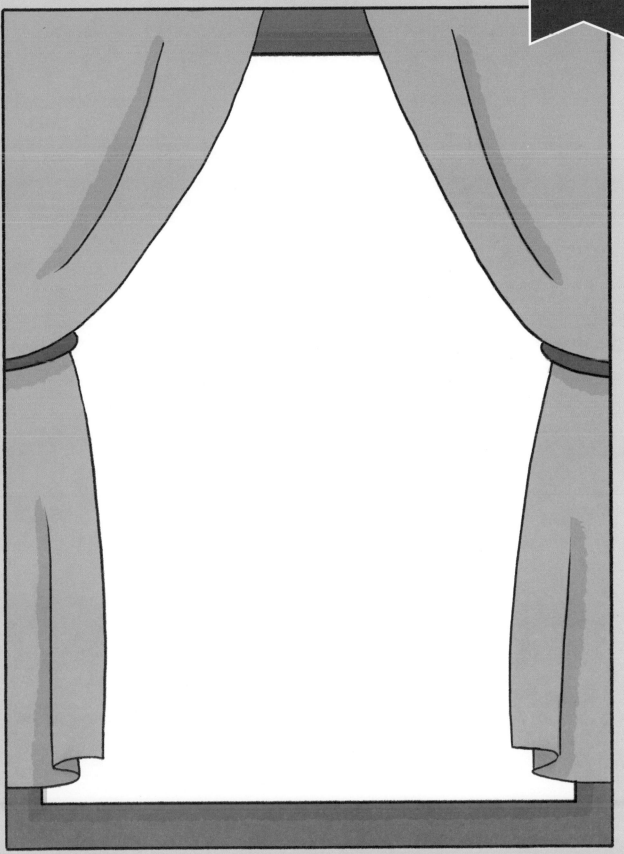

LET'S START! GATHER THESE TOOLS AND MATERIALS.

Piece of string 2–3 feet long	 4–6 cotton balls	 4–6 toothpicks	 Rocks
4–6 craft sticks	 Aluminum foil	 Construction paper	Glue
Tape	 Markers or crayons		 Scissors (with an adult's help)

LET'S TINKER!

Create stars with your materials. Can you combine your stars to form any pictures, like constellations? Which materials can be used to represent the darkness of night?

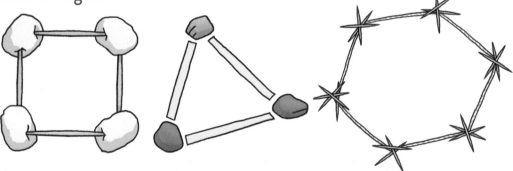

LET'S MAKE: METEORS AND CRATERS!

The surface of the Moon is covered in craters—large and small dents caused by asteroids and meteorites crashing into it.

Find rocks of different sizes and a spot outside with dirt or sand (and no grass) where it is safe to throw rocks.

1. The rocks will be your meteorites—**throw, drop, toss,** and **fling** them at the ground.

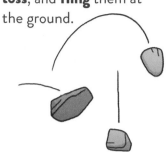

2. Watch what happens when the rocks hit the ground and make craters.

How does the dirt or sand change? That's a crater! Do different rocks make craters that look the same? How can you throw a rock differently to change the size and shape of the craters it makes?

LET'S ENGINEER!

Enid is throwing an ice pop party for her pet spider. She doesn't want the tiny frozen ice pops to melt.

How can Enid keep her ice pops cool on a hot day?

Design something to create shade for the ice pops. How can you use your materials to help? How many spiders and tiny ice pops could fit inside?

PROJECT 3: DONE!
Get your sticker!

Parts of a Plant

Plants have different parts that help them live and grow.

Roots collect water and nutrients, and they hold the plant firmly in the ground.

A **stem** or **trunk** holds the plant or tree up and transports water and nutrients to the leaves, flowers, and fruits.

Leaves collect sunlight and make food for the plant. They also make oxygen.

Flowers grow seeds for the plant.

Fruits provide protection for the seeds. They also help spread the seeds through wind, water, or animals.

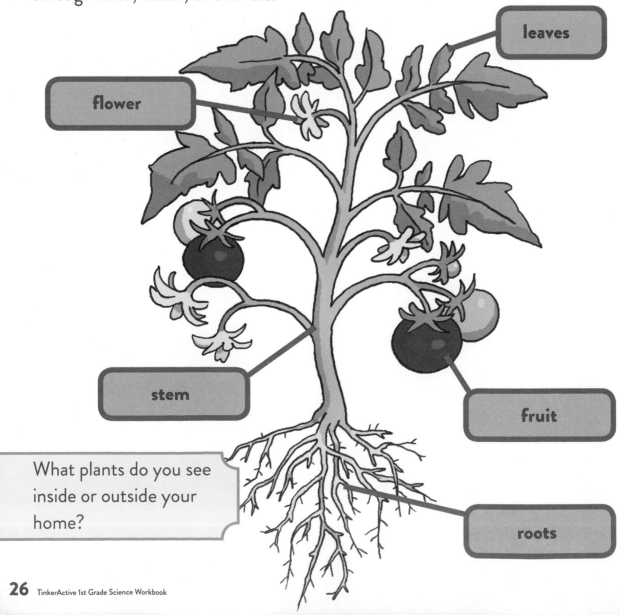

What plants do you see inside or outside your home?

Label the parts of the plants in Brian's garden.

Which parts can you
see on the plants
near you?

Plants use their different parts to help them live and grow in different habitats.

Connect each plant to its habitat.

Bearberry plants have dark leaves and low stems. This helps them absorb heat from the Sun and from Earth so they can survive in very cold temperatures.

Agave leaves have a waxy coating to protect the water inside the plant. This helps them survive in hot habitats with little rainfall.

Bromeliads grow on other plants instead of in the ground. This helps them get closer to the Sun when the plants around them are tall.

Water lilies have stems and leaves that can bend and move. This helps them live in underwater habitats.

RAIN FOREST

FRESH WATER

DESERT

TUNDRA

Look at how each plant uses its parts to live and grow. Then design your own solution to each problem.

A peanut shell protects the seeds inside.

Write about and draw a solution you can use to protect your lunch on the way to school.

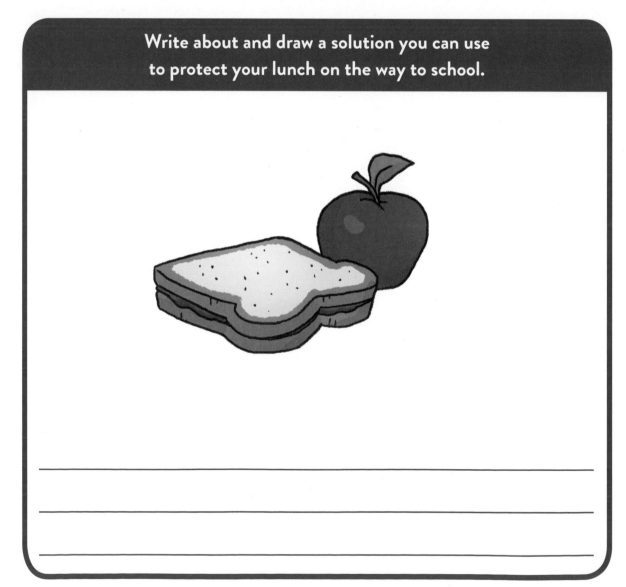

_____

_____

_____

A tree's branches hold the leaves up high to get light from the Sun.

Write about and draw a solution you can use to hold a wet swimsuit and towel up to the Sun to dry.

_____

_____

_____

LET'S START! GATHER THESE TOOLS AND MATERIALS.

 Tape or glue	 4–6 twist ties	 Aluminum foil

 4–6 cotton swabs	 Paper towel tube	 1 paper towel	4–6 paper cups

Spoon	 Scissors (with an adult's help)	 Markers

LET'S TINKER!

Play with your materials to create pictures or sculptures of plant parts. Can you **make** seeds, fruits, leaves, flowers, roots, and a stem or trunk?

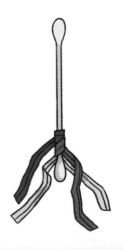

LET'S MAKE: RAINBOW ROOTS!

1. Fill a cup halfway with water.

2. Take a paper towel and **cut** off a narrow strip.

3. Draw a rainbow on the paper towel strip with markers.

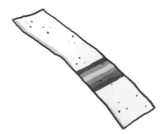

4. Fold the paper towel strip in half and **place** it over a spoon balanced on top of the cup. The ends of the paper towel should dip into the water.

5. Watch what happens. How does the paper towel change? Feel the paper towel—what do you notice? What happens to the water in the cup?

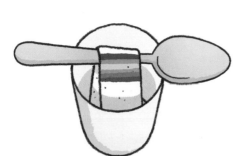

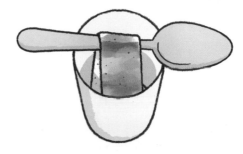

LET'S ENGINEER!

Dimitri is constructing a toy castle and he wants to add a tower. But Dimitri's tower keeps falling over! He knows that the stem and trunk hold a plant up, and the roots hold it firmly in the ground.

How can he build a tower that won't fall over?

Design a tower that stands strong and tall, just like some plants do. Which materials can help you build it taller? Which can help you build it stronger?

Try putting your tower on a table and then shaking the table. Is your tower still standing? If not, build it stronger.

PROJECT 4: DONE!
Get your sticker!

Plant Growth

Plants are living things. They need light, air, water, and nutrients from the dirt to live and grow. Help Dimitri water his plants with the watering can. Draw a line through the maze to visit each plant.

What are other ways that plants can get the water they need to survive?

_____

_____

Plants all need the same things to live, whether they are growing indoors or outdoors. Color each plant's light source **yellow**. Color each plant's water source blue. Color each plant's nutrient source brown.

Plants respond to changes in their environment to keep getting the things they need to live and grow. Draw how each plant changes to meet its needs.

The kapok tree needs lots of light, so it grows taller than the trees around it to gather more sunlight. Draw the tree taller.

The tulip plant needs its pollen to make seeds, so it closes its petals to protect its pollen when it rains. Draw a tulip plant closed.

The spruce tree needs water. During a drought, when there is very little rain, the roots grow deeper to find the water the tree needs.
Draw the roots deeper.

This indoor fern needs sunlight, so it grows toward the window to get more light. Draw the fern's leaves growing closer to the window.

Plants change as they grow, but they continue to look similar to their parent.

These leaves blew away in the wind. Observe and compare them to the trees. Draw a line to connect each leaf to the type of tree it belonged to.

OAK　　　　**BIRCH**　　　　**MAPLE**

Which pairs of leaves come from the same type of tree? Color each pair of leaves the same color.

Go on a leaf hunt around your home or neighborhood. Write about or draw the leaves that you find. Do any of your leaves come from the same kinds of trees?

LET'S START!

3-5 sticks

3-5 leaves

Large paper cup

Construction paper

Crayons

3-5 twist ties

Aluminum foil

Tape

Scissors
(with an adult's help)

LET'S TINKER!

Look closely at your materials. Which come from living things, and which come from nonliving things? Which materials used to grow, and which have always been the same?

Break or **tear** pieces off some of your materials. What's on the inside? How are the insides of living things different from the insides of nonliving things?

LET'S MAKE: POLLEN-FILLED FLOWERS!

Some flowers close at night or in the rain to keep their pollen safe and dry. **Make** your own flower that can open to allow insects to reach the pollen and close to keep the pollen safe.

1. **Take** one stick or **tie** a bunch of sticks together with twist ties.

2. Tape leaves to the bottom or **make** your own leaves by cutting them out of construction paper.

3. Tear or **cut** out pieces of the aluminum foil to make flower petals you can bend open and closed. **Tape** them to the top.

4. Create pollen by cutting the construction paper, foil, or leaves into tiny pieces and hiding them inside your petals.

LET'S ENGINEER!

Callie has a few small plants in her cup. They have dirt, air, and water, but Callie's plants keep dying!

How can Callie keep her plants alive?

Use your cup and some leaves to show how you would plant something so it had all it needed to survive. Is Callie's plant missing light, air, water, or dirt? **Test** your solution by a window to see if your plant is getting all four. Is light able to make it to your leaves?

PROJECT 5: DONE!
Get your sticker!

Plant Life Cycle

All plants can produce more young plants. In the plant life cycle below, circle the seed sprouting into a new young plant.

Not all plants grow from seeds. Some plants, like ferns and mosses, grow from spores!

Write the numbers 1, 2, 3, 4, and 5 to put the life cycle of each plant in order from youngest to oldest.

WATERMELON PLANT

PEA PLANT

Many plants grow seeds inside their fruits. You can eat the fruits, then plant the seeds.

Circle the seeds inside of each fruit.

peach

kiwi

cantaloupe

cherry

orange

apple

avocado

Go to your kitchen. What fruit or vegetable can you bite into to see some seeds?

Read the poem aloud. Then label the parts of the seed.

Seeds

A seed is the start of a new plant,
with all it needs to survive.
Seeds can be any shape or size—
any color of seed will thrive!

The **seed coat** wraps the seed up tight,
protecting what's inside.
The **endosperm** is just beneath,
holding food for the seed's ride.

The most important part of the seed
we've saved for very last.
The **embryo** is wrapped up safe,
its cells ready to start growing fast.

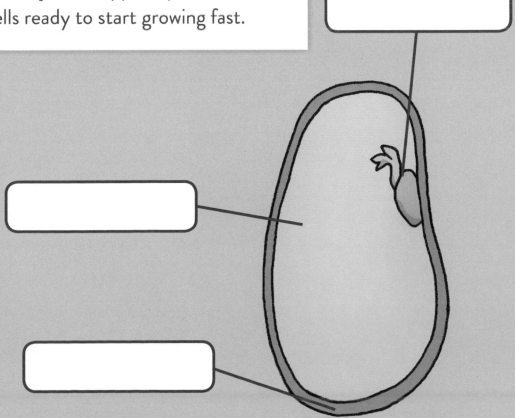

Seeds travel in different ways. Some travel in the wind. Some travel when animals eat them and carry them to new places.

sunflower

maple

willow

apple

dandelion

rosewood

blackberry

acorn

Look at the seeds on page 46. Then fill in the chart with the seeds that you predict travel in the wind and the seeds that you predict are eaten by animals.

How Do Seeds Move?

In the Wind	Eaten by Animals
rosewood	apple

When you pick a dandelion and blow on it, what happens? Go outside, find another seed, and draw it.

LET'S START!

4–6 cotton balls

Paper

Crayons or markers

Scissors
(with an adult's help)

Tape

Aluminum foil

4–6 rubber bands

4–6 paper clips

LET'S TINKER!

Many seeds grow inside of fruits, like apples. Other seeds grow on the outside of fruits, like strawberries.

Look at your materials. Which could look like the seeds inside a fruit? Which could look like the seeds outside a fruit? Try to **re-create** both types of seeds.

LET'S MAKE: SPINNING SEEDS!

Seeds move in different ways in the wind. They can float, fly, drop, glide, or even spin. **Make** your own spinning seed like a helicopter!

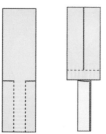

1. **Cut** and **fold** the template on page 48 as shown. Cut on the solid lines. Fold on the dashed lines.

2. **Use** one of your materials, like a rubber band or paper clip, as a weight on the bottom.

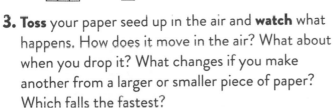

3. **Toss** your paper seed up in the air and **watch** what happens. How does it move in the air? What about when you drop it? What changes if you make another from a larger or smaller piece of paper? Which falls the fastest?

LET'S ENGINEER!

Frank wants to send a secret note to Dimitri, who is sitting across the room.

How can he get the note to Dimitri quickly and quietly?

Design a solution to move a note through the air like a seed. **Start** with a note written on a large or small piece of paper. How can you fold or cut the paper to help it move? Which other materials can you use to help the message fly, glide, or spin? How far can your note travel?

PROJECT 6: DONE!
Get your sticker!

Types of Animals

There are two types of animals: vertebrates and invertebrates. Vertebrates are animals with backbones, like cows. Invertebrates are animals without backbones, like bees.

Draw a line to match each vertebrate to its description.

I am a mammal who has pointed ears and whiskers.

I am called a "bird of prey" because of my hunting skills. I live high up in a nest made of sticks.

I can move in the water and on land. I don't need to drink water because I absorb it through my skin.

hawk

frog

cat

I ♥ MY CAT

Draw a line to match each invertebrate to its description.

snail

I live in water. I have five arms, and if I lose one, I can grow a new one.

I am an arachnid. I make silk and spin webs.

starfish

I make a hard shell to live in.

spider

Read about the types of vertebrates. Then draw a line to connect each animal to its type.

Reptiles live on land, breathe air, and lay eggs.

Birds have feathers, beaks, and wings.

Fish live in the water. They have gills and scales.

swordfish

Gila monster

Amphibians live in the water and on land, but they do not have any scales.

Mammals are covered in hair and make milk to feed their young.

poison dart frog

bald eagle

zebra

Two types of invertebrates are insects, like an ant, and arachnids, like a tarantula.

All insects have six legs. They also have three important body parts—a head, a middle section called a thorax, and an abdomen. Many insects also have wings.

Add the missing labels for each insect.

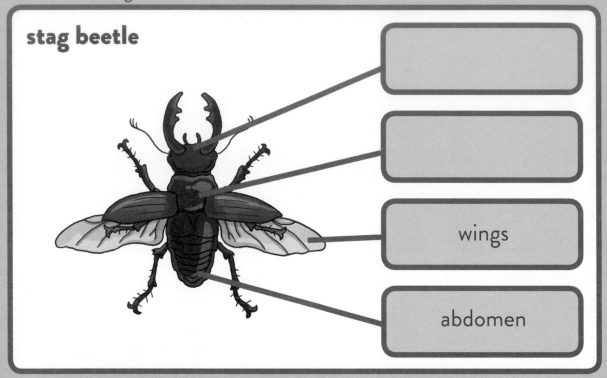

stag beeetle

wings

abdomen

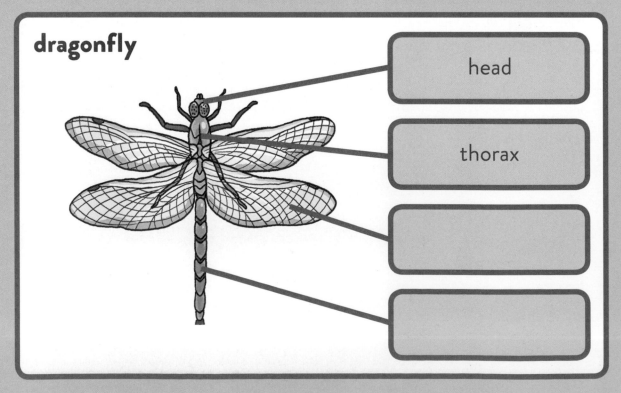

dragonfly

head

thorax

All arachnids have eight legs. They also have two main body parts—an abdomen and a combined head and thorax called a cephalothorax.

Count the legs of each invertebrate. Circle the insects. Then put a square around the arachnids.

scorpion　　　　　**mite**　　　　　**tarantula**

fly　　　　　**grass spider**　　　　　**cockroach**

mouse spider　　　　　**grasshopper**

LET'S START! GATHER THESE TOOLS AND MATERIALS.

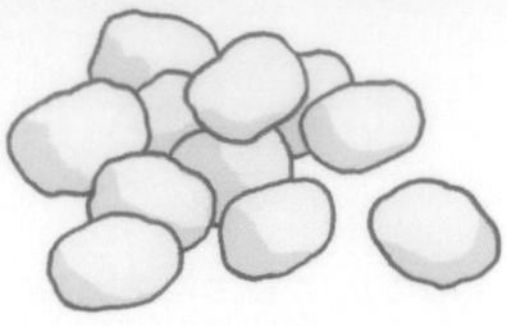
6 or more cotton balls

Tissues

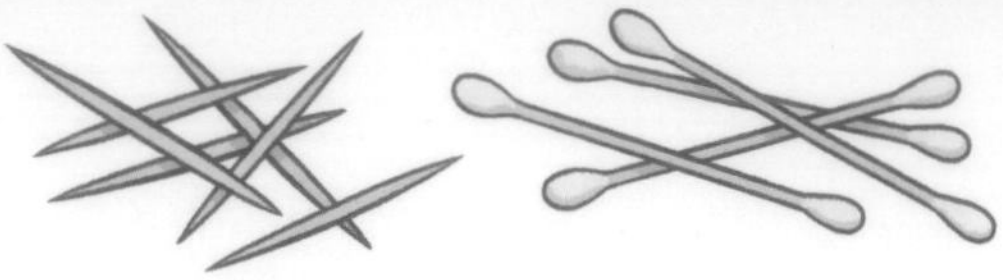
6 or more toothpicks or cotton swabs

Construction paper

Glue

Tape

Paper plate

12 or more pieces of dried pasta

Aluminum foil

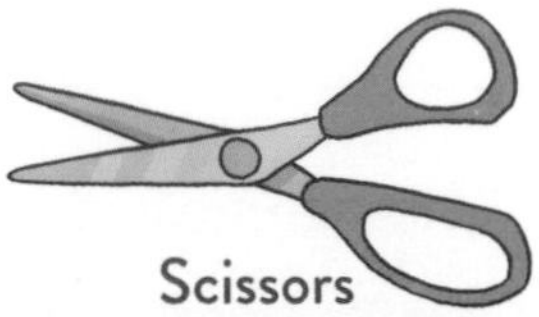
Scissors
(with an adult's help)

LET'S TINKER!

Animals are classified into two types, vertebrates and invertebrates, by whether or not they have a backbone.

Classify and **sort** your materials. Can they be divided into hard and soft groups? Rigid and bendable? Natural and man-made? Dark and light?

LET'S MAKE: SKELETONS!

A vertebrate has a backbone that shapes its body and protects what's inside. The backbone and the body are covered by skin. **Build** your own backbone or skeleton of a human or an animal.

1. Use the toothpicks, cotton swabs, or dried pasta for bones. **Glue** them onto a piece of construction paper.

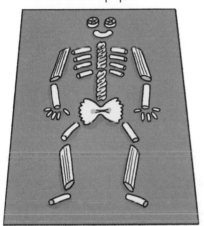

2. Add cottons balls, tissues, or construction paper on top of the bones, like skin. **Name** your skeleton!

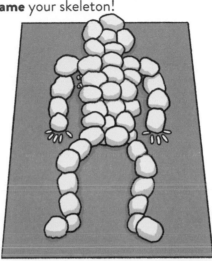

LET'S ENGINEER!

Amelia's crackers often get smashed in her backpack on the way to school.

How can she protect them better?

Design a shell that can protect Amelia's crackers. What materials can cover them? How can you combine or bend the materials to make them stronger?
Test your design.

PROJECT 7: DONE!
Get your sticker!

Animal Babies

All animals have babies. Some lay eggs. Others give birth. Fill in the name of each stage in the life cycle.

egg   hatchling   chick   hen

chicken

Write the numbers 1, 2, 3, and 4 to label the life cycle in order from youngest to oldest.

dog

Some animal babies make noises to let their parents know they need help.

These chirping baby bluebirds are hungry. Draw a line to lead the mother bluebird back to the nest with a worm for her babies to eat.

Some animals don't make noise. How do you think they let their parents know when they need help? How would you let an adult know you needed help without making noise?

_____

People also make noises to communicate.

Write about and draw how you let your parents know when you need something.

_____

_____

_____

Write about and draw how you communicated when you were a baby. Gather information by talking to others in your family.

_____

_____

_____

Young animals can look similar to their parents, but each is still unique.

Draw a line to connect each young shark to its parent.

hammerhead shark

whale shark

tiger shark

thresher shark

Look closely at these young animals and their parents.

Circle the parents and babies that look similar. Cross out the parents and babies that look different.

DOG

TAPIR

FROG

ELEPHANT

LET'S START!

GATHER THESE TOOLS AND MATERIALS.

Construction paper

Scissors
(with an adult's help)

4–6 cotton balls

Beads

Piece of string 2–3 feet long

Plastic wrap

Cereal pieces

Paper cup

Markers

Glue

LET'S TINKER!

Animals, like some birds, reptiles, and even fish, protect their eggs from the weather and predators in a soft but strong nest.

Look at your materials. Which do you think would be the softest? Which do you think would be the strongest?

Build a nest using your materials. **See** what happens when you put something inside the nest.

LET'S MAKE: BUTTERFLY EGGS!

Many butterflies hide their colorful eggs by laying them on the undersides of leaves. **Make** your own colorful collection of butterfly eggs.

1. Cut a leaf shape out of paper.

2. Create some eggs using cotton balls, beads, or cereal pieces.

3. **Color** your eggs with markers if necessary.

4. **Glue** your eggs to the underside of your paper leaf. **Wait** ten minutes for the glue to dry. **Flip** the leaf over!

LET'S ENGINEER!

Enid is taking apples to school to share with her class. She has a bumpy bus ride and wants to keep her apples safe from bruising.

How can she best protect her apples?

Design a way for Enid to safely carry the apples to school. **Use** some of your materials to represent the apples. How many apples can your design carry?

PROJECT 8: DONE!
Get your sticker!

Animal Survival

Some animals have special body parts that help them get the food and water they need.

Chameleons use their long, skinny tongues to catch insects to eat. Their tongues can be up to two times as long as their bodies! Draw the chameleon's tongue.

Woodpeckers have strong bills and sticky tongues to dig insects from deep inside of trees. Draw the woodpecker's tongue.

Try using your tongue to grab food!

Circle the body part that you predict the hummingbird uses to get nectar from a daylily flower.

Circle the body part that you predict the giraffe uses to reach acacia leaves in tall trees.

Some animals also have special body parts that help them see, hear, move, and protect themselves.

Porcupines are covered in sharp quills to protect them from predators like bobcats, wolves, and owls. Draw the porcupine's quills.

Rhinoceroses have cup-shaped ears that can turn to listen in any direction! This helps them hear sounds from far away. Draw the rhinoceros's ears.

Circle the body part that you predict the elephant uses for making noise.

Circle the body part that you predict the turtle uses to walk on land and swim quickly in the water.

People can learn from animals and how they use their special body parts to survive.

Look at how this painted turtle buries himself in the sand and mud when he wants to go to sleep.

Write about and draw how you could go to sleep when it is too bright in your room.

Look at how these arctic bumblebees shiver and move in order to warm up in the cold.

Write about and draw how you could keep warm in the cold.

LET'S START!

GATHER THESE TOOLS AND MATERIALS.

4–6 sticks

4–6 toothpicks

Modeling clay or mud

Plastic wrap

Aluminum foil

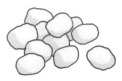
4–6 cotton balls

Ice cube

LET'S TINKER!

Many animals use special body parts to get the food they need. An elephant uses its trunk to lift food to its mouth, and a butterfly uses its proboscis, a special feeding tube, to drink nectar.

Look at your materials. Which can you use to move things, grab things, and pick things up? Which can you use to push or pull with?

LET'S MAKE: COLD PROTECTOR!

Many animals survive in the cold by having layers of fat or blubber or thick fur. **Experiment** to see which materials protect you from the cold.

1. Grab a piece of plastic wrap and an ice cube. **Lay** the plastic wrap on your palm (like skin). **Place** the ice cube on the plastic wrap. What does it feel like? How does the feeling change the longer you hold the ice?

2. Choose a layer of protection for your hand, like a lump of clay or some cotton balls. Then **lay** the plastic wrap over it. **Place** the ice on the plastic wrap again, this time with the layer of protection between your hand and the ice. What does it feel like? How does it compare to when you held the ice with no protection?

3. Experiment with different materials from around your home, like a sweater, paper towels, or even feathers. Which ones protect you from the cold the best?

LET'S ENGINEER!

Callie is caught in a hailstorm, and the hail really hurts! (Hail is small clumps of ice and snow that fall like rain.)

How can she protect herself?

Design a protective layer for Callie. How can your materials be used to protect her from the hail?

PROJECT 9: DONE!
Get your sticker!

Five Senses

People have five senses to help them experience their environment. You can hear, see, taste, touch, and smell.

Draw a line to answer each question.

What body part do you use to hear your friend talking?

What body part do you use to see your homework?

What body part do you use to taste a snack?

What body part do you use to touch a friendly pet?

What body part do you use to smell a flower?

You taste with your tongue. Circle the tastes that you like.

Draw on the plate the foods that are your favorite to taste.

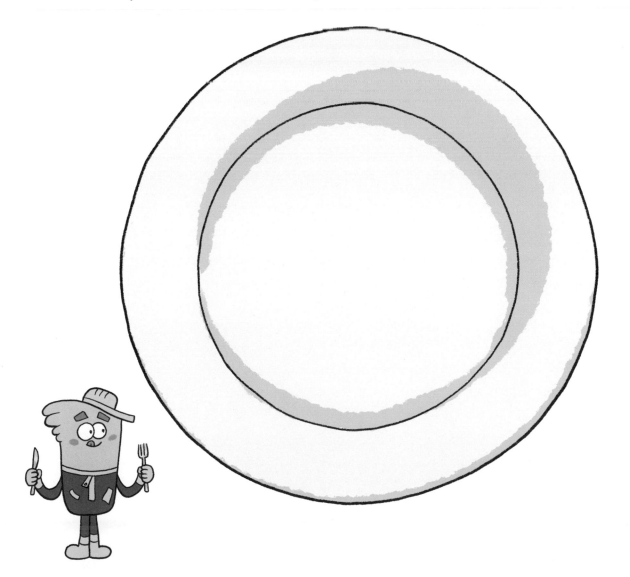

You smell with your nose. Draw a line to connect each thing to the words "good smell" or "bad smell."

good smell

bad smell

What is your favorite smell? Draw it.

Your ears help you hear if sounds are loud or soft.
Write the word "loud" or "soft" under each picture.

_____

_____

_____

_____

_____

_____

You touch things with the skin on your hands and on the rest of your body.

Draw a line to connect each picture to a word that describes how it feels.

rough   **cold**   **soft**

Cross out the pictures of things you shouldn't touch.

You see with your eyes. The iris of an eyeball can be many different colors. Color this iris to match yours.

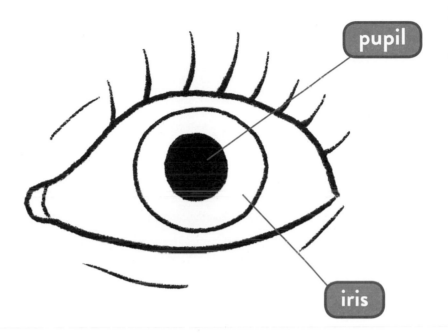

Look around the room you're in. Draw a picture of what you see.

LET'S START! GATHER THESE TOOLS AND MATERIALS.

Shoebox

Assorted materials like:
chalk, rubber bands, short pieces of
string, paper clips, rocks, cotton balls,
cereal pieces, dried fruit

Clothespin

Spoon

Bowl

Vinegar

Flour

Vegetable or
coconut oil

LET'S TINKER!

Use your five senses to explore your materials.

Describe what each one feels, looks, sounds, and smells like. Are any safe to taste?

Can you **change** how any of them look, feel, smell, or sound when you hold or combine them?

LET'S MAKE: SENSORY SAND!

Make a mixture to explore with your senses!

1. Pour four cups of flour and ½ cup of oil into a bowl.

2. Mix the flour and oil with a spoon or your hands until it is fully combined.

3. Use your senses to explore!

4. Record your findings on this chart:

 What does the mixture look like?

 What does it sound like?

 What does it feel like?

 What does it smell like?

 Ask an adult if it is safe to taste. If so, what does it taste like?

LET'S ENGINEER!

The MotMots are going on a field trip to the orange orchard, but Amelia doesn't like the smell of oranges.

How can she go on the trip without having to smell the oranges?

Design something to safely block her sense of smell using your materials.

Test your design with different smells.

PROJECT 10: DONE!
Get your sticker!

Energy

Anything that moves uses energy. Light, sound, and heat are forms of energy. Circle the items below that use energy.

Anything that moves uses energy.

Anything that lights up uses energy.

Anything that heats up uses energy.

Anything that makes noise uses energy.

Energy can make things move and change. Read the story aloud.
Circle the main type of energy Callie uses in each picture.

Callie loves camp! She swims in the lake.

| light | movement | sound | heat |

She plays songs with her friends.

| light | movement | sound | heat |

She roasts a snack over the campfire.

light movement sound heat

She reads under the stars using a flashlight.

light movement sound heat

There is energy all around us. Take a walk inside or outside your home and look for things that use energy.

Write about and draw something that lights up.

_____

Write about and draw something that makes noise.

_____

Write about and draw something that moves.

_____

_____

Write about and draw something that heats up.

_____

_____

LET'S START!

Paper

Dice

Paper towel tube

4–6 cotton balls

Markers or crayons

LET'S TINKER!

When things are in motion, they're using energy.

Move your materials around to see what they're like when they are in motion. What happens when you drop, push, or pull them? Which materials can roll and which can bounce? What is moving these objects?

LET'S MAKE: LIGHT MAP!

1. **Draw** a map of your home with markers or crayons on a piece of paper.

2. **Add** the sources of light that keep your home bright. You can **use** stickers from page 129 or draw them with your markers or crayons.

3. When it's dark out, **turn** the lights off.

Is there still some light? If so, where is the light coming from? **Add** any other sources of light that you've noticed to your map.

Do you use the same sources of light during the day and at night?

LET'S ENGINEER!

Enid's art project turned into a mess, and fast. She wants to move her markers off the table to keep them clean, but her hands are covered in paint!

How can Enid move the markers without touching them?

Design a tool to get the markers off the table without touching them with your hands.

PROJECT 11: DONE!
Get your sticker!

Sound

Sound is a form of energy you can hear.

Draw how Dimitri can experiment with each of these things to make sound.

Sound is made when something vibrates. The vibrations make sound waves that move through the air.

Circle the part of the guitar that vibrates to make sound.

Inside your throat, your vocal cords vibrate to make sound, too. Circle the vocal cords that are vibrating.

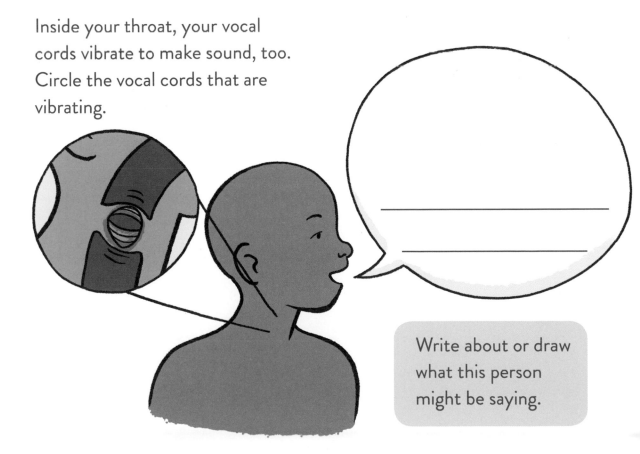

Write about or draw what this person might be saying.

Sounds have a volume. They can be loud or soft.

Circle the sounds that are usually quiet.

What do you think makes the loudest sound on this page?

_____

Why do you think it needs to be loud? _____

_____

_____

Listen to the sounds around you right now. Then write about and draw what you hear. Think of as many as you can.

Circle the sound that is the loudest.
Put a box around the sound that is the closest to you.
Is the loudest sound also the one closest to you?

_____

_____

Sounds travel at different speeds through different materials. This can change the way something sounds.

Write a description of the sound you would hear in each picture. Then circle the sound in each row you predict would be louder.

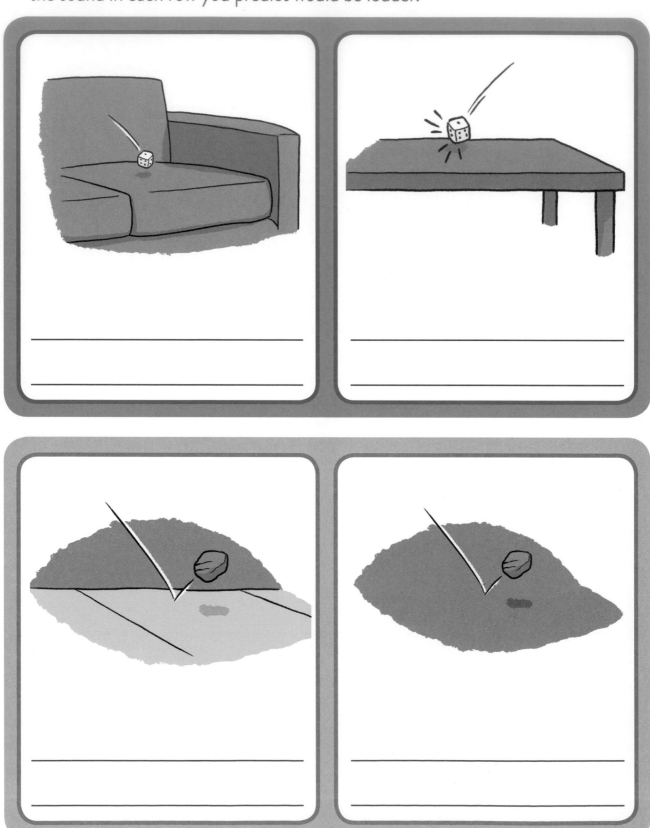

Drop your pencil on this book.
Next drop your pencil on the floor.
Write about and draw which sound was quieter.

Find another surface where you can experiment with dropping the pencil—
maybe a table, a carpet, or a chair. Write about and draw what you hear.

LET'S START! GATHER THESE TOOLS AND MATERIALS.

5 or more rubber bands

Piece of string
4–5 feet long

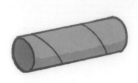

Toilet paper tube

Paper cups

5 or more coins

Spoon

LET'S TINKER!

Pick up each of your materials. What sounds can you make with them?

Tap each one on the floor, on your leg, and on a table. Does the sound change? What happens if you combine materials?

Think about how you can use your materials to make other noises. Can you make sounds that are softer or louder?

Touch your throat while you hum or sing. Can you feel your vocal cords vibrating? Do any of your materials vibrate?

LET'S MAKE: SOUND OBSERVER!

All sounds are made when something vibrates. **Make** a tool to carry vibrations right to your ears!

1. **Tie** the middle of a long piece of string around a metal spoon.

2. Wrap the ends of the string a few times around your two index fingers, then **stick** your fingers into your ears.

3. Experiment with swinging the spoon gently into objects around you. The string is carrying vibrations from the spoon right to your fingers and into your eardrums! What does it sound like? Do hard and soft objects make different kinds of sounds? How does the sound change when you swing the spoon gently? How about quickly?

LET'S ENGINEER!

Brian has been busy cooking a special meal for his family. Now it's time for dinner, but his dinner bell is broken.

How can Brian let everyone know that it's time to eat—without using his voice?

Build an instrument Brian can play to call his family to dinner.

PROJECT 12: DONE!
Get your sticker!

Light is a form of energy you can see. Some things give off their own light. Color those things yellow.

Some things can only be seen with a light source.

Draw a light source you use in your room at night.

Draw how your room looks.

Draw a light source you use in your room during the day.

Draw how your room looks.

Look around the space you are in. What light source is closest to you?

Light moves in a straight line. Draw beams of light from each of the three light sources in the picture.

Read the story aloud. Then add details to the picture showing what you think Brian saw under the bed.

It was very late and dark at the sleepover. All of Brian's friends were sleeping. Brian heard a noise in the dark. Then he heard it again! Brian got his flashlight out of his backpack. He snuck over to the bed and slowly peeked underneath it. Then he flipped on his flashlight!

Many kinds of balls bounce.

Draw how you think this ball will bounce.

When a beam of light hits a shiny surface, like a mirror, it also bounces. This is called reflection.

Draw how you think the light of the flashlight will reflect.

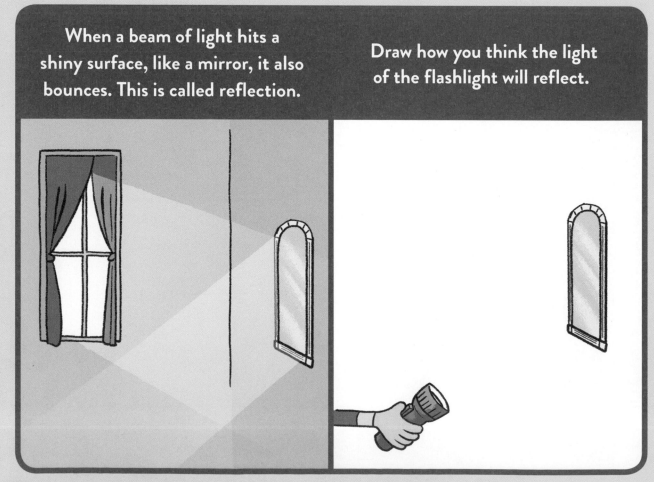

You can use a mirror to redirect a beam of light. You can also see your reflection.

Stand in front of a mirror in your home. Draw what you see.

Circle the shiny things that can reflect light.

LET'S START!

GATHER THESE TOOLS AND MATERIALS.

 Flashlight	 Pencil, crayon, or marker	Construction paper	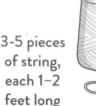 Scissors (with an adult's help)	 Tape
Aluminum foil	 Spoon	 4–6 twist ties	Clothes hanger	3-5 pieces of string, each 1–2 feet long

LET'S TINKER!

Look at your materials and predict which ones will reflect light.

Use the flashlight to shine a beam of light onto each item. Which items reflect the light? How can you tell? Were your predictions correct?

Turn all the lights off. Does anything change?

Discover other materials in your home that reflect light.

LET'S MAKE: FLASHLIGHT PICTURES!

1. **Place** your flashlight facedown first on a piece of paper. **Trace** it with a pencil, crayon, or marker to make a circle.

2. **Cut** out the paper circle. Then **cut** out or **poke** a few holes in the circle.

3. Tape the paper circle over the lens of the flashlight and turn it on. **Point** the flashlight at the wall, floor, or ceiling to project your pattern!

LET'S ENGINEER!

It's time for Amelia's party, but she doesn't have a disco ball. A disco ball reflects light around a room in fun shapes and patterns! Amelia can't have a party without something like a disco ball.

How can you help save the day with a similar decoration?

Build your own hanging party decoration that reflects light in fun shapes and patterns.

PROJECT 13: DONE!
Get your sticker!

Shadows

Some materials allow a lot of light to pass through them. Other materials allow only a little light to pass through them.

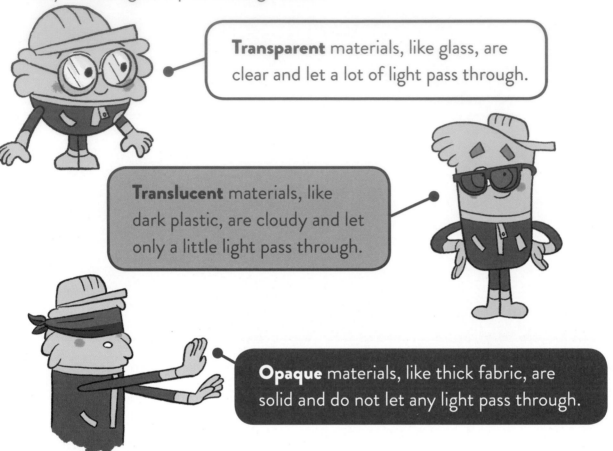

Transparent materials, like glass, are clear and let a lot of light pass through.

Translucent materials, like dark plastic, are cloudy and let only a little light pass through.

Opaque materials, like thick fabric, are solid and do not let any light pass through.

Draw what you see when you look through a pair of sunglasses.

Look around your home. What other translucent materials do you see? Try looking through them!

Draw what you think the flashlight's light rays will do when they hit these objects. Then circle whether each one is transparent, translucent, or opaque.

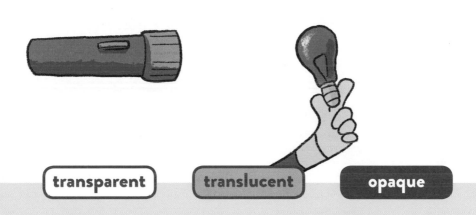

transparent   **translucent**   **opaque**

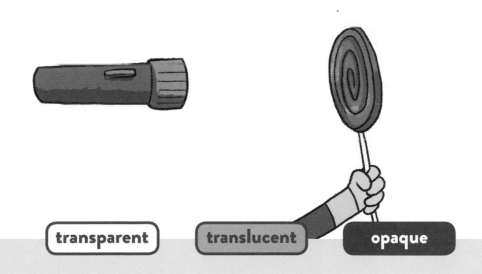

transparent   **translucent**   **opaque**

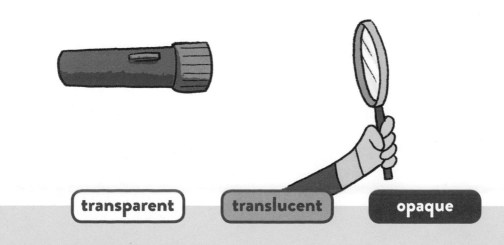

transparent   **translucent**   **opaque**

A shadow is made when light is blocked by an opaque object. Read the poem aloud. Then draw a shadow behind each MotMot and decorate it.

> Shadow, shadow, on the wall,
> who's the funniest of them all?
> Shadows short and shadows tall,
> watch them dance until nightfall.

Look around your home. What other opaque materials do you see?
Try making shadows with them on this page!

Shadows create shade, which helps to keep the area in the shadows cool.

The MotMots are playing outside on a hot day. Draw the shadows in each picture that will keep the MotMots cool.

Should the MotMots choose the sun or the shade?
Circle one word below.

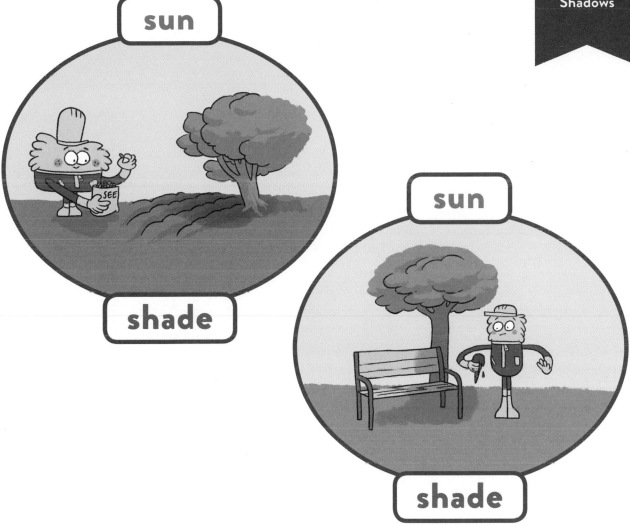

sun

shade

sun

shade

Take a walk around the inside or outside of your home and find a place where you can make a shadow.

What light source will you use?

_____

What does your shadow look like?

_____

LET'S START!

Flashlight

Paper

Aluminum foil

Toilet paper tube

Plastic wrap

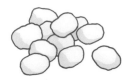

4–6 cotton balls

Collection of toy animals, action figures, or dolls

LET'S TINKER!

Hold your materials in front of a flashlight or a sunny window one at a time. Can you make shadows with them? Do the shadows move? Do any of the materials not make shadows?

Move the materials close to the light, then far away from it. How do the shadows change?

Combine the materials and see what happens.

Think about other light sources you can use to make shadows.

LET'S MAKE: SHADOW SHOW!

1. **Make** a shadow shape of an animal or a person with your materials or hands.

2. **Use** a light source like a flashlight or a sunny window to project your shadow character onto the floor or wall.

3. **Move** your shadow character around.

4. **Make** other shadow shapes to create a story with your shadow character. **Combine** the materials to make shadows of different shapes and sizes. **Try** making more than one shadow at a time.

LET'S ENGINEER!

The MotMots are having a beach party, and Callie has a special delivery for them. However, she doesn't know where to land her hot-air balloon.

How can Callie figure out where to land?

Design a solution with your materials to make a shadow **X** on the ground where Callie can land.

PROJECT 14: DONE!
Get your sticker!

Light & Sound

Light and sound can be used to communicate with other people, even from far away. Circle the things you've seen and/or heard.

lighthouse

fire engine

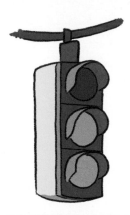

traffic light

ambulance

bell

dog

Look around your home. What do you see that makes light or sound?

Fill in the diagram with the objects from page 114 that fall into each category. Which ones communicate with light, with sound, or with both light and sound?

Ways to Communicate

signal wands

`light`

fire alarm

`light and sound`

`sound`

yelling

People use sound to communicate in many ways.

Circle the pictures of the MotMots communicating using sound.

Draw a picture of how you communicate using sound.

Many animals communicate using sound, too.

Read the poem aloud. Then draw a picture of how a rattlesnake communicates.

Rattlesnake Shake

A rattlesnake has no ears you can see,
so it cannot hear like you or like me.
But it still uses sound as it slithers around
to scare predators in the air and on the ground.

When an eagle, coyote, or whip snake comes by,
this snake will hold its rattle up high.
The sound of its shaker says, "Do not come near!"
And those who hear should soon disappear.

People also use light to communicate in many ways.
Write a ✓ under "yes" or "no" for each item in the chart.

Does this item communicate with light?

alarm clock	YES	NO

life vest	YES	NO

car	YES	NO

trumpet	YES	NO

caution light	YES	NO

Traffic lights communicate important information.

 means **GO** and means **STOP**.

Trace a line through the maze to the movie theater. Drive only on roads with a .

THE MOTMOT MOVIE

LET'S START! GATHER THESE TOOLS AND MATERIALS.

Spoon

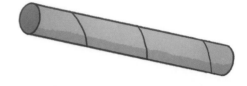
Glue stick

Pencil

Drinking straw

Paper towel tube

LET'S TINKER!

Tap each of your materials on a table, on the floor, and on one another. What sounds can you make? Are your sounds loud or soft?

Play around to create your own pattern with sounds. Which sounds repeat?

LET'S MAKE: SECRET CODE!

Many of the ways that we communicate use patterns.

1. **Create** your own secret code using sound patterns.

2. Use the chart below to keep track of your sound patterns.

Sound	Sound	Sound	Sound
1 loud tap	3 quiet claps		
Meaning	Meaning	Meaning	Meaning

LET'S ENGINEER!

Frank is going to the movie theater with his mom. He knows that he's not allowed to talk while the movie is playing, but he may get hungry or thirsty before it's over.

How can Frank tell his mom what he needs without talking?

Design an object for Frank to take in his pocket to communicate.

Or **think** of a way he can communicate with just his body.

PROJECT 15: DONE!
Get your sticker!

ANSWER KEY

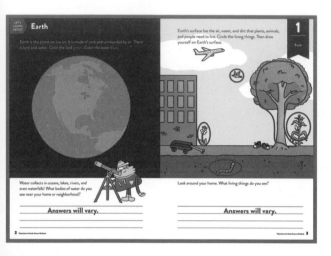

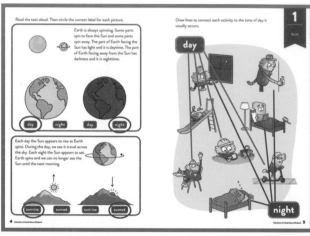

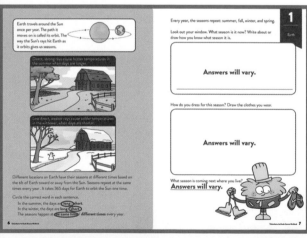

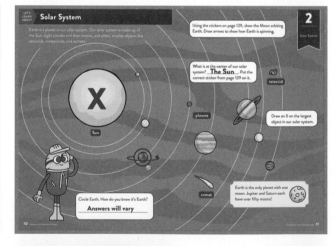

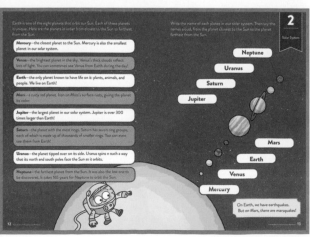

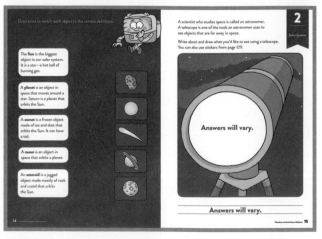

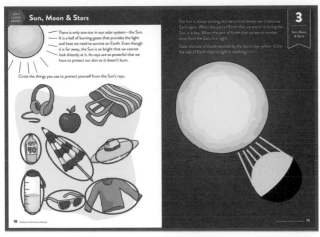

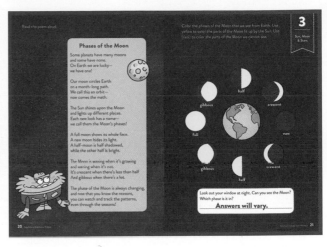

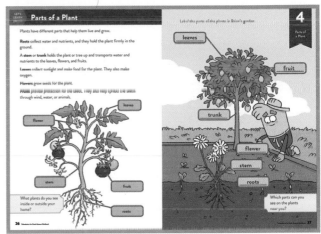

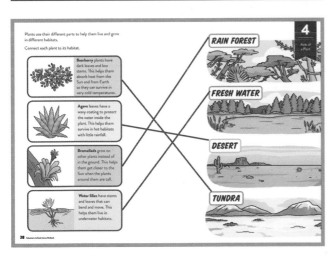

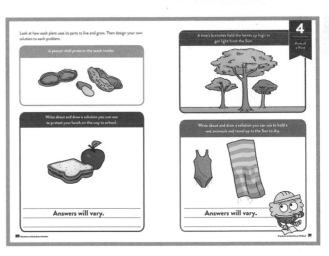

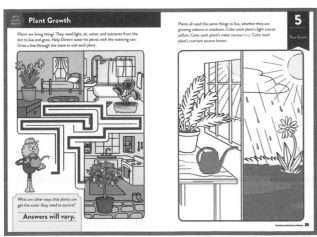

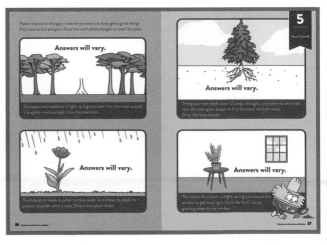

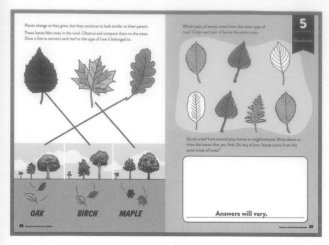

Plants change as they grow, but they continue to look similar to their parent. These leaves blew away in the wind. Observe and compare them to the trees. Draw a line to connect each leaf to the type of tree it belonged to.

OAK   BIRCH   MAPLE

5
Plant Growth

Which pairs of leaves come from the same type of tree? Color each pair of leaves the same color.

Go on a leaf hunt around your home or neighborhood. Write about or draw the leaves that you find. Do any of your leaves come from the same kinds of trees?

Answers will vary.

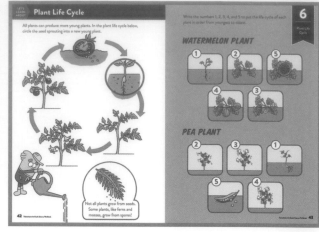

LET'S LEARN ABOUT
Plant Life Cycle

All plants can produce more young plants. In the plant life cycle below, circle the seed sprouting into a new young plant.

Not all plants grow from seeds. Some plants, like ferns and mosses, grow from spores!

6
Plant Life Cycle

Write the number 1, 2, 3, 4, and 5 to put the life cycle of each plant in order from youngest to oldest.

WATERMELON PLANT

PEA PLANT

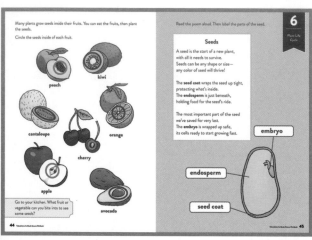

Many plants grow seeds inside their fruits. You can eat the fruits, then plant the seeds.

Circle the seeds inside of each fruit.

peach   kiwi
cantaloupe   orange
cherry
apple   avocado

Go to your kitchen. What fruit or vegetable can you bite into to see some seeds?

6
Plant Life Cycle

Read the poem aloud. Then label the parts of the seed.

Seeds

A seed is the start of a new plant,
with all it needs to survive.
Seeds can be any shape or size—
any color of seed will thrive!

The **seed coat** wraps the seed up tight,
protecting what's inside.
The **endosperm** is just beneath,
holding food for the seed's ride.

The most important part of the seed
we've saved for very last.
The **embryo** is wrapped up safe,
its cells ready to start growing fast.

embryo
endosperm
seed coat

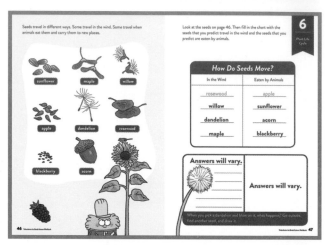

Seeds travel in different ways. Some travel in the wind. Some travel when animals eat them and carry them to new places.

sunflower   maple   willow
apple   dandelion   rosewood
blackberry   acorn

6
Plant Life Cycle

Look at the seeds on page 46. Then fill in the chart with the seeds that you predict travel in the wind and the seeds that you predict are eaten by animals.

How Do Seeds Move?

In the Wind	Eaten by Animals
rosewood	apple
willow	sunflower
dandelion	acorn
maple	blackberry

Answers will vary.   **Answers will vary.**

When you pick a dandelion and blow on it, what happens? Go outside, find another seed, and draw it.

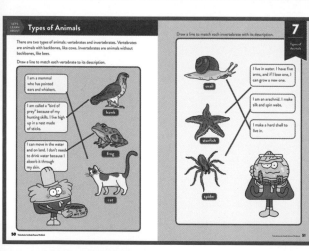

LET'S LEARN ABOUT
Types of Animals

There are two types of animals: vertebrates and invertebrates. Vertebrates are animals with backbones, like cows. Invertebrates are animals without backbones, like bees.

Draw a line to match each vertebrate to its description.

I am a mammal who has pointed ears and whiskers.

I am called a "bird of prey" because of my hunting skills. I live high up in a nest made of sticks.

I can move in the water and on land. I don't need to drink water because I absorb it through my skin.

hawk
frog
cat

7
Types of Animals

Draw a line to match each invertebrate with its description.

snail
starfish
spider

I live in water. I have five arms, and if I lose one, I can grow a new one.

I am an arachnid. I make silk and spin webs.

I make a hard shell to live in.

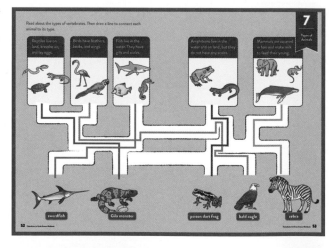

Read about the types of vertebrates. Then draw a line to connect each animal to its type.

Reptiles live on land, breathe air, and lay eggs.

Birds have feathers, beaks, and wings.

Fish live in water. They have gills and scales.

Amphibians live in the water and on land, but they do not have dry scales.

Mammals are covered in hair and make milk to feed their young.

7
Types of Animals

swordfish   Gila monster   poison dart frog   bald eagle   zebra

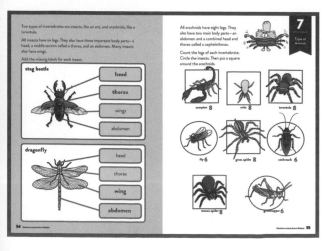

Two types of invertebrates are insects, like an ant, and arachnids, like a tarantula.

All insects have six legs. They also have three important body parts—a head, a middle section called a thorax, and an abdomen. Many insects also have wings.

Add the missing labels for each insect.

stag beetle
head
thorax
wings
abdomen

dragonfly
head
thorax
wing
abdomen

7
Types of Animals

All arachnids have eight legs. They also have two main body parts—an abdomen and a combined head and thorax called a cephalothorax.

Count the legs of each invertebrate. Circle the insects. Then put a square around the arachnids.

scorpion 8   mite 8   tarantula 8
fly 6   grass spider 8   cockroach 6
recluse spider 8   grasshopper 6

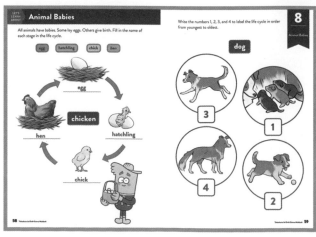

LET'S LEARN ABOUT
Animal Babies

All animals have babies. Some lay eggs. Others give birth. Fill in the name of each stage in the life cycle.

egg   hatchling   chick   hen

egg
chicken
hen   hatchling
chick

8
Animal Babies

Write the numbers 1, 2, 3, and 4 to label the life cycle in order from youngest to oldest.

dog
3
1
4
2

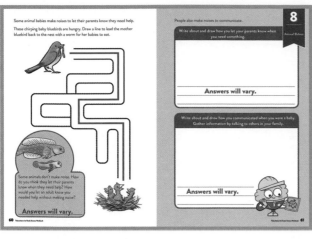
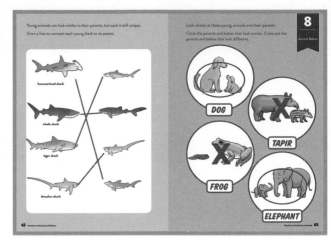
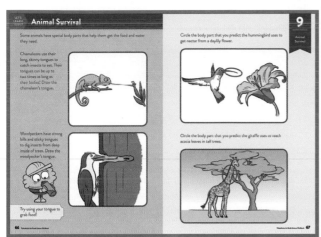
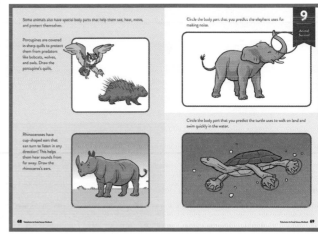
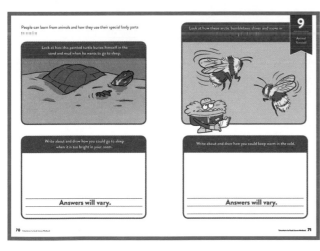
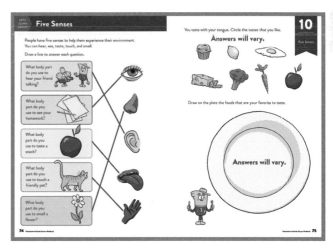
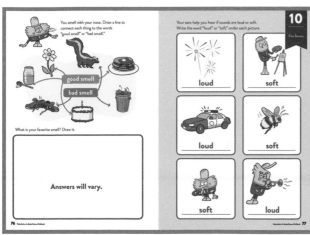
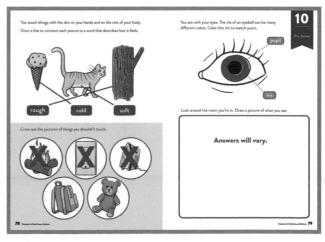

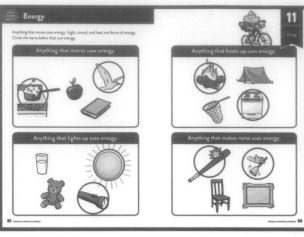

Energy

Anything that moves uses energy. Light, sound, and heat are forms of energy. Circle the items below that use energy.

- Anything that moves uses energy.
- Anything that heats up uses energy.
- Anything that lights up uses energy.
- Anything that makes noise uses energy.

11 · Energy

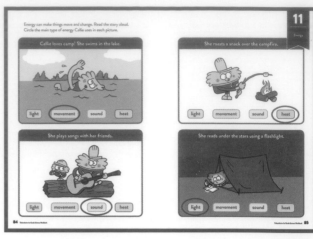

Energy can make things move and change. Read the story aloud. Circle the main type of energy Callie uses in each picture.

Callie loves camp! She swims in the lake. — light / **movement** / sound / heat

She roasts a snack over the campfire. — light / movement / sound / **heat**

She plays songs with her friends. — light / movement / **sound** / heat

She reads under the stars using a flashlight. — **light** / movement / sound / heat

11 · Energy

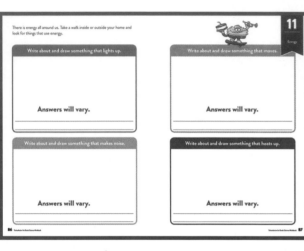

There is energy all around us. Take a walk inside or outside your home and look for things that use energy.

- Write about and draw something that lights up. — Answers will vary.
- Write about and draw something that moves. — Answers will vary.
- Write about and draw something that makes noise. — Answers will vary.
- Write about and draw something that heats up. — Answers will vary.

11 · Energy

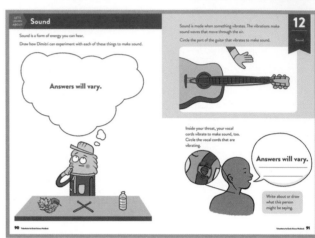

Sound

Sound is a form of energy you can hear. Draw how Dimitri can experiment with each of these things to make sound. — Answers will vary.

Sound is made when something vibrates. The vibrations make sound waves that move through the air. Circle the part of the guitar that vibrates to make sound.

Inside your throat, your vocal cords vibrate to make sound, too. Circle the vocal cords that are vibrating. — Answers will vary.

Write about or draw what this person might be saying.

12 · Sound

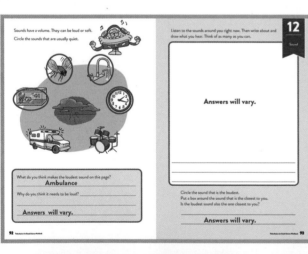

Sounds have a volume. They can be loud or soft. Circle the sounds that are usually quiet.

What do you think makes the loudest sound on this page? — Ambulance

Why do you think it needs to be loud? — Answers will vary.

Listen to the sounds around you right now. Then write about and draw what you hear. Think of as many as you can. — Answers will vary.

Circle the sound that is the loudest. Put a box around the sound that is the closest to you. Is the loudest sound also the one closest to you? — Answers will vary.

12 · Sound

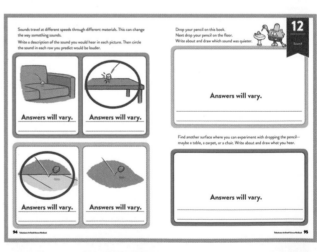

Sounds travel at different speeds through different materials. This can change the way something sounds. Write a description of the sound you would hear in each picture. Then circle the sound in each row you predict would be louder. — Answers will vary.

Drop your pencil on this book. Next drop your pencil on the floor. Write about and draw which sound was quieter. — Answers will vary.

Find another surface where you can experiment with dropping the pencil—maybe a table, a carpet, or a chair. Write about and draw what you hear. — Answers will vary.

12 · Sound

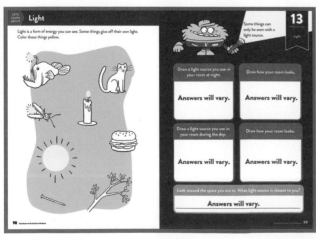

Light

Light is a form of energy you can see. Some things give off their own light. Color those things yellow.

Some things can only be seen with a light source.

- Draw a light source you use in your room at night. — Answers will vary.
- Draw how your room looks. — Answers will vary.
- Draw a light source you use in your room during the day. — Answers will vary.
- Draw how your room looks. — Answers will vary.

Look around the space you are in. What light source is closest to you? — Answers will vary.

13 · Light

Light moves in a straight line. Draw beams of light from each of the three light sources in the picture.

Read the story aloud. Then add details to the picture showing what you think Brian saw under the bed.

It was very late and dark at the sleepover. All of Brian's friends were sleeping. Brian heard a noise in the dark. Then he heard it again! Brian got his flashlight out of his backpack. He snuck over to the bed and slowly peeked underneath it. Then he flipped on his flashlight!

Answers will vary.

13 · Light

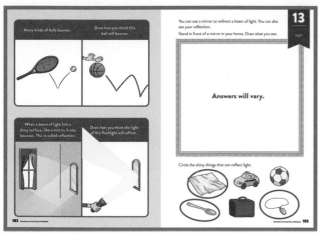
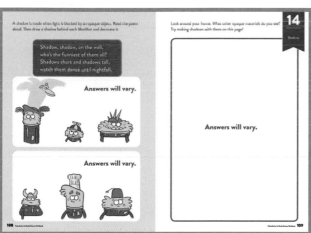
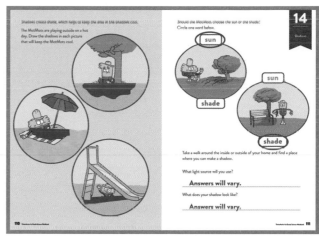
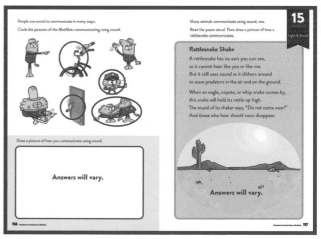
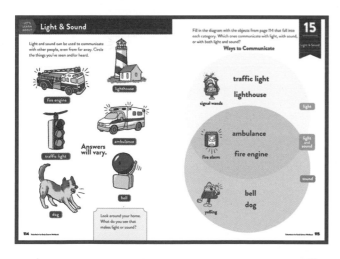
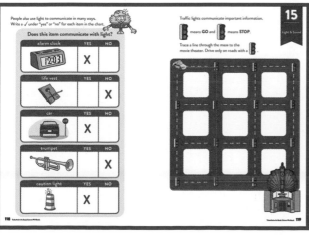
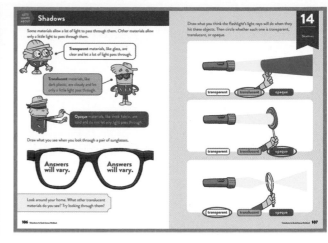

Odd Dot
175 Fifth Avenue
New York, NY 10010
OddDot.com

ISBN: 978-1-250-30725-5

WRITER   Megan Hewes Butler

ILLUSTRATORS   Lauren Pettapiece, Les McClaine, and Chad Thomas

EDUCATIONAL CONSULTANT   Amanda Raupe

CHARACTER DESIGNER   Anna-Maria Jung

COVER ILLUSTRATOR   Anna-Maria Jung

BACK COVER CHARACTER ILLUSTRATOR   Chad Thomas

BADGE EMBROIDERER   El Patcha

INTERIOR DESIGNER   Phil Conigliaro

COVER DESIGNERS   Carolyn Bahar and Colleen AF Venable

EDITOR   Justin Krasner

Our books may be purchased in bulk for promotional, educational, or business use. Please contact your local bookseller or the Macmillan Corporate and Premium Sales Department at (800) 221-7945 ext. 5442 or by email at MacmillanSpecialMarkets@macmillan.com.

DISCLAIMER
The publisher and authors disclaim responsibility for any loss, injury, or damages that may result from a reader engaging in the activities described in this book.

TinkerActive is a trademark of Odd Dot.
Printed in China by Hung Hing Off-set Printing Co. Ltd., Heshan City, Guangdong Province
First edition, 2019

10 9 8 7 6 5 4 3 2 1

For the activity on page 15

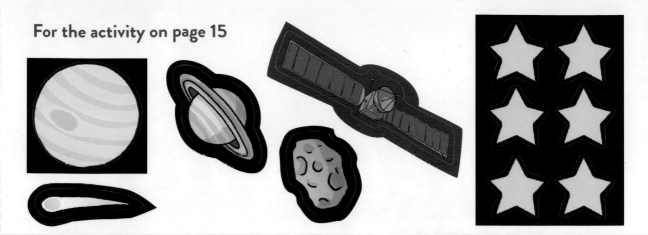

For the activity on page 10–11

For the activity on page 88

Sticker your *TINKERACTIVE EXPERT* poster after you complete each project.

_____
(Your Name Here)

IS A TINKERACTIVE EXPERT!

PLACE YOUR MATH BADGE HERE!

PROJECT 1
PROJECT 2
PROJECT 3
PROJECT 4
PROJECT 5
PROJECT 6
PROJECT 7
PROJECT 8
PROJECT 9
PROJECT 10
PROJECT 11
PROJECT 12
PROJECT 13
PROJECT 14
PROJECT 15

PLACE YOUR SCIENCE BADGE HERE!

PROJECT 1
PROJECT 2
PROJECT 3
PROJECT 4
PROJECT 5
PROJECT 6
PROJECT 7
PROJECT 8
PROJECT 9
PROJECT 10
PROJECT 11
PROJECT 12
PROJECT 13
PROJECT 14
PROJECT 15

PLACE YOUR ENGLISH LANGUAGE ARTS BADGE HERE!

PROJECT 1
PROJECT 2
PROJECT 3
PROJECT 4
PROJECT 5
PROJECT 6
PROJECT 7
PROJECT 8
PROJECT 9
PROJECT 10
PROJECT 11
PROJECT 12
PROJECT 13
PROJECT 14
PROJECT 15

 COLLECT THEM ALL!